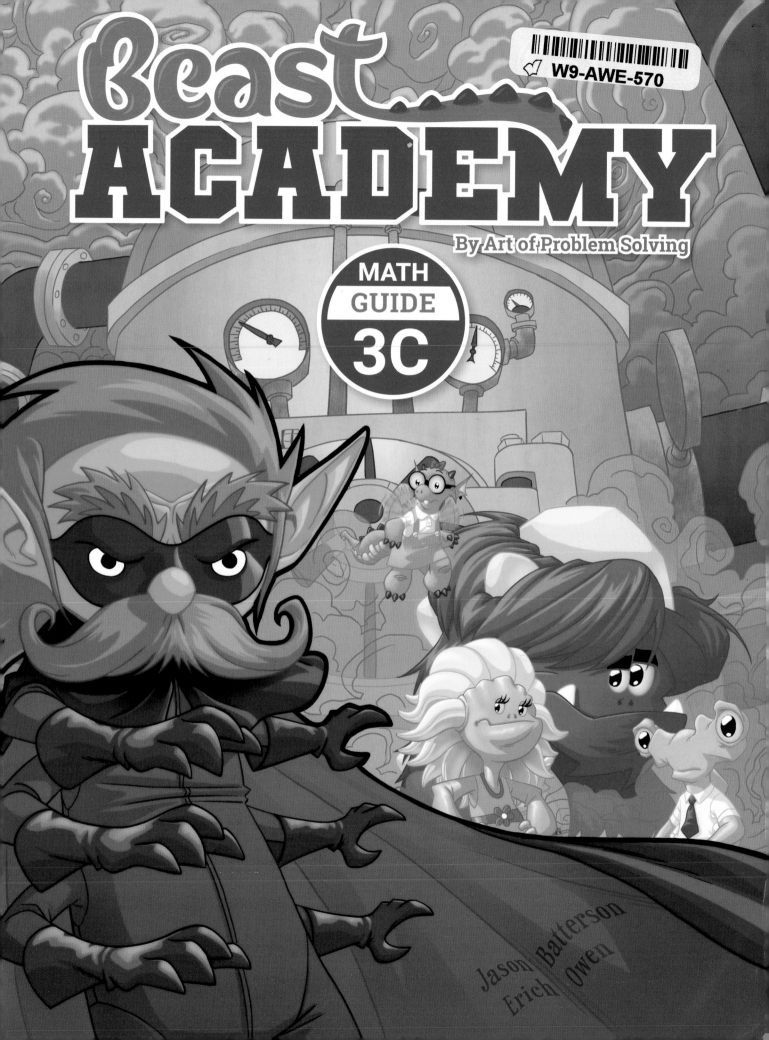

Published by: AoPS Incorporated
                     10865 Rancho Bernardo Rd Ste 100
                     San Diego, CA 92127-2102
                     info@BeastAcademy.com

ISBN: 978-1-934124-44-4

Written by Jason Batterson
Illustrated by Erich Owen
Colored by Greta Selman

Visit the Beast Academy website at BeastAcademy.com.
Visit the Art of Problem Solving website at artofproblemsolving.com.
Printed in the United States of America.
2020 Printing.

Become a Math Beast!
For additional books,
printables, and more, visit
BeastAcademy.com

This is Guide 3C in the Beast Academy level 3 series:

Contents:

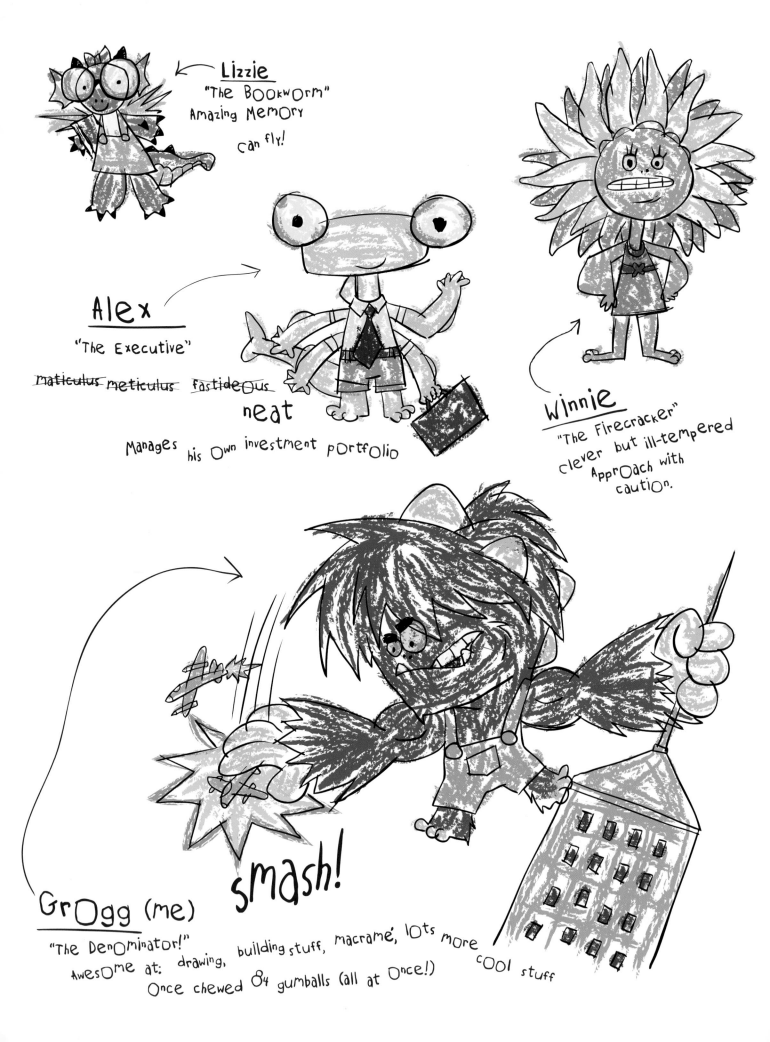

Lizzie
"The Bookworm"
Amazing Memory

Can fly!

Alex
"The Executive"
~~maticulus~~ ~~meticulus~~ ~~fastideous~~
neat

Manages his own investment portfolio

Winnie
"The Firecracker"
clever but ill-tempered
Approach with caution.

smash!

Grogg (me)
"The Denominator!"
Awesome at: drawing, building stuff, macramé, lots more cool stuff
Once chewed 84 gumballs (all at once!)

sergeant Rote
senior Drill Instructor (Gym Teacher)
hide and seek champion

Professor Grok
math lab
easily abducted by "Calamitous Clod"

ms. Q
math teacher
always has extra supplies
faster than she looks

breathes under water

Captain Kraken
shop teacher (ex-pirate)
"spins yarns" about "plunderin"

krak!

Mr. Wriggles

Rosencrantz and Guildenstern
custodians custodian custodians
hard to remember who is who
once, when Ralph threw up in class, they put sawdust on it.

Fiona
math team coach
knows lots of cool tricks
soccer team captain

Welcome to Beast Academy!

This book is called the Guide.

There is also a separate Practice book with lots of problems you can use to sharpen your skills.

The Guide is written like a comic book.

In a comic book, whatever I say shows up in these bubbles. They're called comic balloons.

Here's one!

Each character has a different balloon color. This makes it easy to tell who is talking.

My balloons are purple!

The story is told in panels.

Panels usually have a rectangular frame around them...

...like this one.

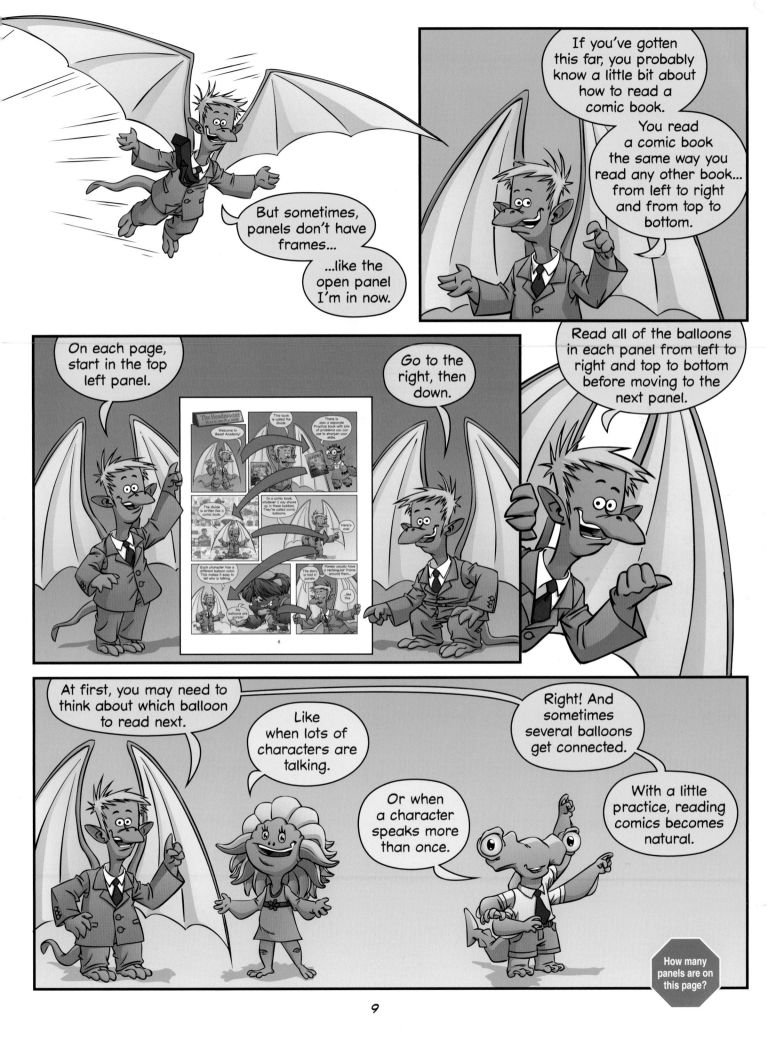

Contents: Chapter 7

See page 6 in the Practice book for a recommended reading/practice sequence for Chapter 7.

Chapter 7: Variables

R & G
n

Do you have a favorite number?

I do.

Mine is 42. What's yours?

n.

?!? Your favorite NUM-ber.

I told you, my favorite number is n.

Today's program was brought to you by the letter n.

Letter n

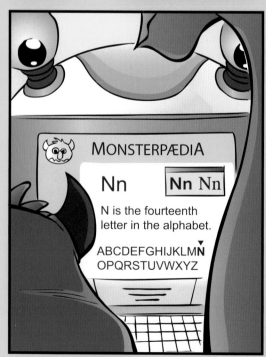

MONSTERPÆDIA

Nn   Nn Nn

N is the fourteenth letter in the alphabet.

ABCDEFGHIJKLM**N**
OPQRSTUVWXYZ

n is a *letter*.

Sure. Math beasts use letters all the time.

What for?

Letters can stand for **numbers**... n can be **any** number!

?!?

Alphabet DUMM...

14

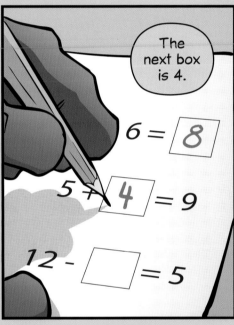

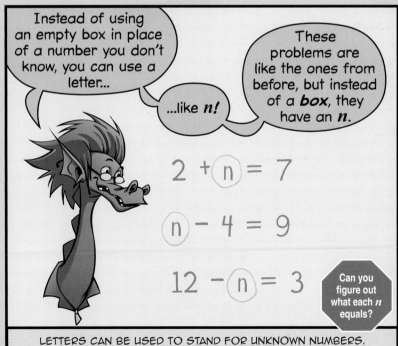

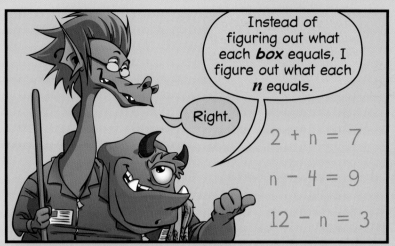

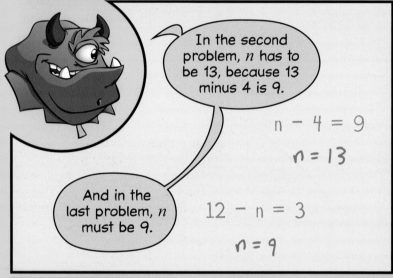

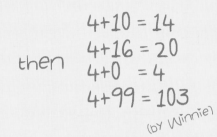

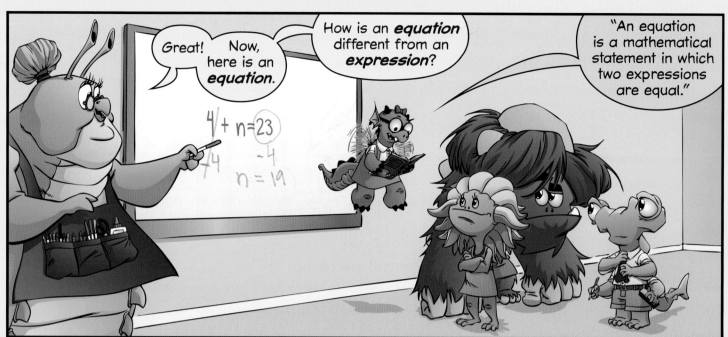

Great! Now, here is an **equation**.

How is an **equation** different from an **expression**?

"An equation is a mathematical statement in which two expressions are equal."

$4 + n = 23$

$-4 \quad -4$

$n = 19$

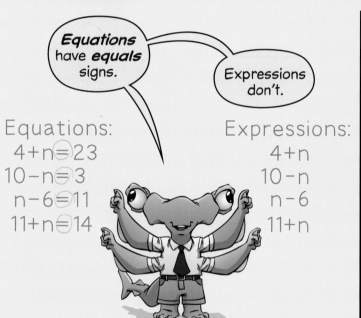

Equations have **equals** signs.

Expressions don't.

Equations:
$4 + n = 23$
$10 - n = 3$
$n - 6 = 11$
$11 + n = 14$

Expressions:
$4 + n$
$10 - n$
$n - 6$
$11 + n$

In an **equation**, we can figure out what number the variable is!

FIGURING OUT WHAT NUMBER A VARIABLE REPRESENTS IN AN EQUATION IS CALLED **SOLVING** THE EQUATION. THE NUMBER THAT THE VARIABLE REPRESENTS IS THE **SOLUTION** TO THE EQUATION.

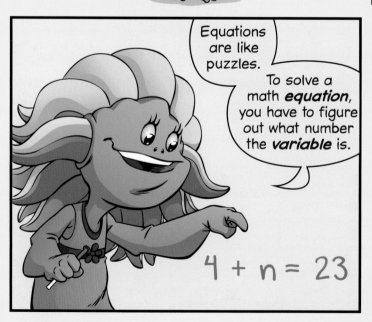

Equations are like puzzles.

To solve a math **equation**, you have to figure out what number the **variable** is.

$4 + n = 23$

For example, if $4 + n = 23$, then n is 19, because $4 + 19 = 23$.

$4 + n = 23$

$4 + 19 = 23$ ✓

so $n = 19$

20

$$10 - n = 3$$

$$n - 6 = 11$$

$$11 + n = 14$$

Solve all three.

21

Practice: Pages 7-11

Simplifying Expressions

Winnie

Original Expression	Simplified Expression	
6−3	3	Simplify just means
16+4	20	to write the expression
5+6−2+1−9	1	in an easier way.
4×9+2×4	44	

Original Expression	Simplified Expression	
6−6	0	When you subtract
7−7	0	a number from itself,
28−28	0	you always get zero.
n−n	0	So, n−n is 0

Original Expression	Simplified Expression	
6+1−1	6	Adding a number and
17+5−5	17	subtracting the same
12+n−n	12	number is the same as
n+7−7	n	doing nothing.

Original Expression	Simplified Expression	
4+4+4+4+4	5×4 (or 20)	It's usually simpler
7+7+7+7	4×7 (or 28)	to write repeated
n+n+n+n+n+n	6×n	addition as
(n+5)+(n+5)+(n+5)	3×(n+5)	multiplication.

Original Expression	Simplified Expression	
6+197−6	197	more examples.
33+w−33	w	
16+43−43−16	0	
h+j−j−h	0	
3+3+3+3−3−3−3	3	
m+m+m+m−m−m−m	m	

Do any of you speak another language?

I know a little Monchhichi.

I learned some Snork last summer.

I speak Smurf.

Draconic! All dragons speak it.

Great! When you know two languages, you can translate from one language into the other.

What we are learning today is a lot like translating. We are going to turn **words** into **math**. Let's start by writing some equations for these sentences that include variables.

Nine minus x is 4.

The product of eight and j is thirty-two.

If you subtract 17 from c, you get 15.

Try to write an equation for each.

Nine minus x is 4.

$$9 - x = 4$$

Nailed it!

"Product" means you are **multiplying** eight and j...

...and the word "is" means equals.

The product of eight and j is thirty-two.

$$8 \times j = 32$$

24

These next problems are a little harder. You need to choose a variable to represent the unknown number.

Seven more than a number is 31.

Five times Dugg's age is 35.

Mick needs three more points to reach 100.

Try to write an equation for each.

Seven more than a number is 31.

7 plus n is 31

$7 + n = 31$

For the first sentence, we can use *n* to represent the number.

So, 7 plus *n* is 31.

For the second sentence, we can use *d* for Dugg's age.

Five times Dugg's age is 35.

5 times d is 35

$5 \times d = 35$

For the last sentence, *m* can represent the number of points that Mick has.

If he gets 3 more, he will have 100.

So, $m + 3 = 100$.

Mick needs three more points to reach 100.

m plus 3 is 100

$m + 3 = 100$

Great!

It's usually a good idea to choose variables that help you remember what each represents...

...like *n* for a number, *d* for Dugg's age, and *m* for Mick's points.

26

Writing and Solving Equations   Lizzie

Nine minus x is 4.
equation: $9 - x = 4$
  Since $9 - \boxed{5} = 4$
    $x = 5$

The product of 8 and j is 32.   product means multiply
equation: $8 \times j = 32$
         $8 \times \boxed{4} = 32$
            $j = 4$

If you subtract 17 from c, you get 15. $30 \xrightarrow{+2} \boxed{32}$
  equation: ~~17 - c~~ $c - 17 = 15$ $- 17 \quad \boxed{- 17}$
                  $\boxed{32} - 17 = 15$ $13 \xrightarrow{+2} \boxed{15}$
                    $c = 32$

59 is 18 less than w. $80 \xrightarrow{-3} \boxed{77}$
equation: $w - 18 = 59$ $- 18 \quad \boxed{- 18}$
          $\boxed{77} - 18 = 59$ $62 \xrightarrow{-3} \boxed{59}$
              $w = 77$

7 more than a number is 31.   the variable n represents a number
  equation: $7 + n = 31$
           $7 + \boxed{24} = 31$
              $n = 24$

5 times Dugg's age is 35.   d represents Dugg's age (in years)
  equation: $5 \times d = 35$
           $5 \times \boxed{7} = 35$
              $d = 7$

Mick needs 3 more points to reach 100.   m is the number of points
  equation: $m + 3 = 100$ Mick has now
           $\boxed{97} + 3 = 100$
              $m = 97$

30

Guessin' and checkin' can be useful... ...but there always be more than one way to solve a problem.

I got the answer with a drawing!

If we add fifteen coins to the sack, that makes 204 coins.

So, if we take fifteen coins away from 204, we get the number of coins that are in the sack.

You just subtract fifteen from 204! It's the same answer we got by guessing and checking!

$$\begin{array}{r} 204 \\ -15 \\ \hline 189 \end{array}$$

Excellent figurin'! How can we make Grogg's doodle into a proper math equation?

Write an equation that matches Grogg's drawing.

31

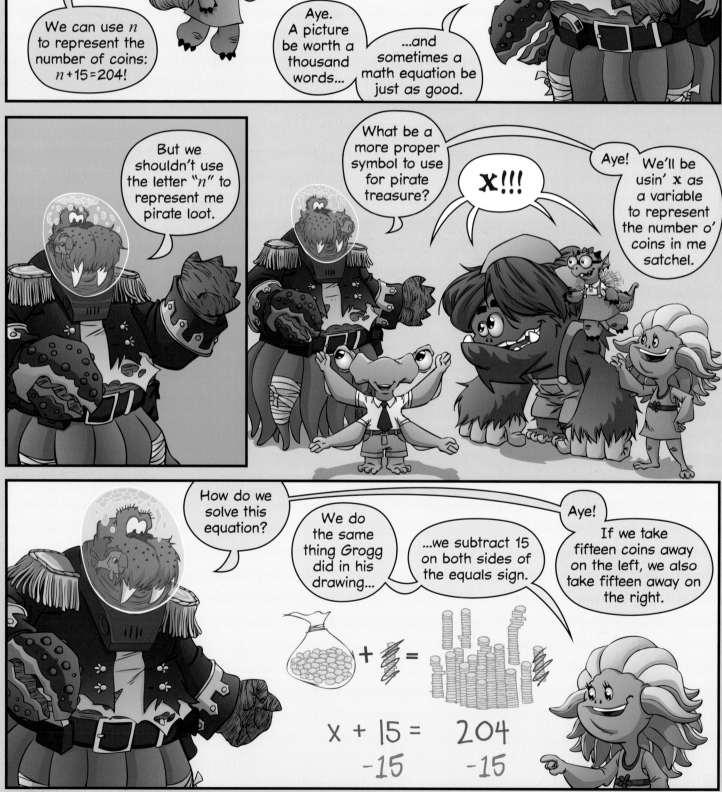

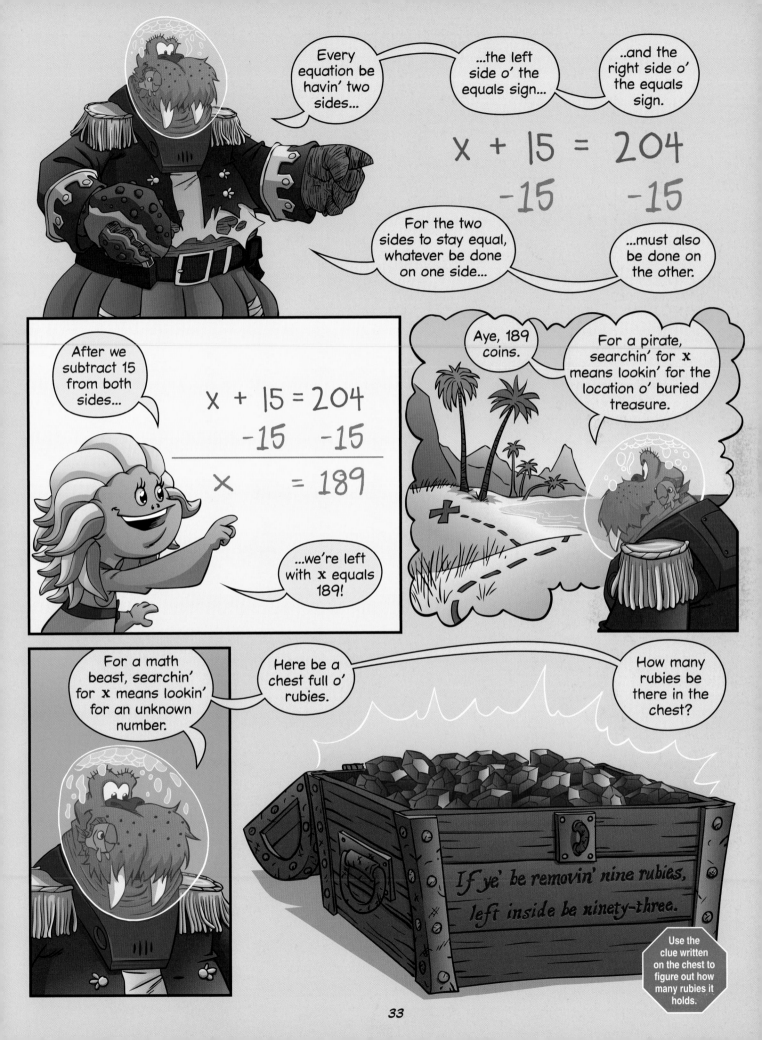

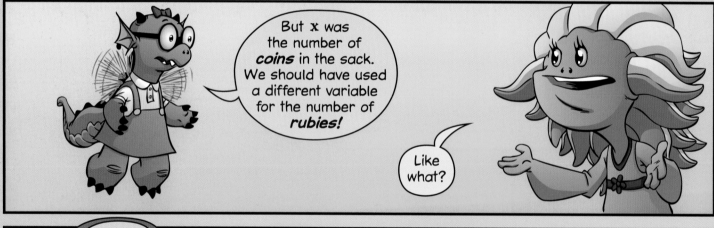

Wild
Tic-tac-toe

Standard Tic-tac-toe:

Tic-tac-toe is a popular game for two players played with pencil and paper. The game begins with a standard 3×3 board as shown below.

Players take turns placing X's and O's on the board. In standard tic-tac-toe, one player places the X's and the other places the O's. The player who gets three of his or her marks in a line (horizontally, vertically, or diagonally) is the winner. If all the spaces on the board are filled and neither player has three in a row, the result is a draw (tie).

Below is an example of a standard game of tic-tac-toe in which the first player (Lizzie, marking X's) wins.

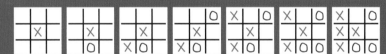

If both players play perfectly, a game of standard tic-tac-toe will always end in a draw.

Wild Tic-tac-toe:

Wild tic-tac-toe is a variation of standard tic-tac-toe with one important difference. On each turn, a player may choose to place an X or an O. The player to complete a line of three X's or three O's is the winner.

Below is an example of a game of wild tic-tac-toe won by the first player.

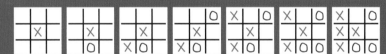

The first player can always win a game of wild tic-tac-toe if he or she plays correctly. Can you find a strategy that will allow you to win every time if you play first?

Find a partner and play!

IT'S ALWAYS A GOOD IDEA TO CHECK YOUR ANSWER!

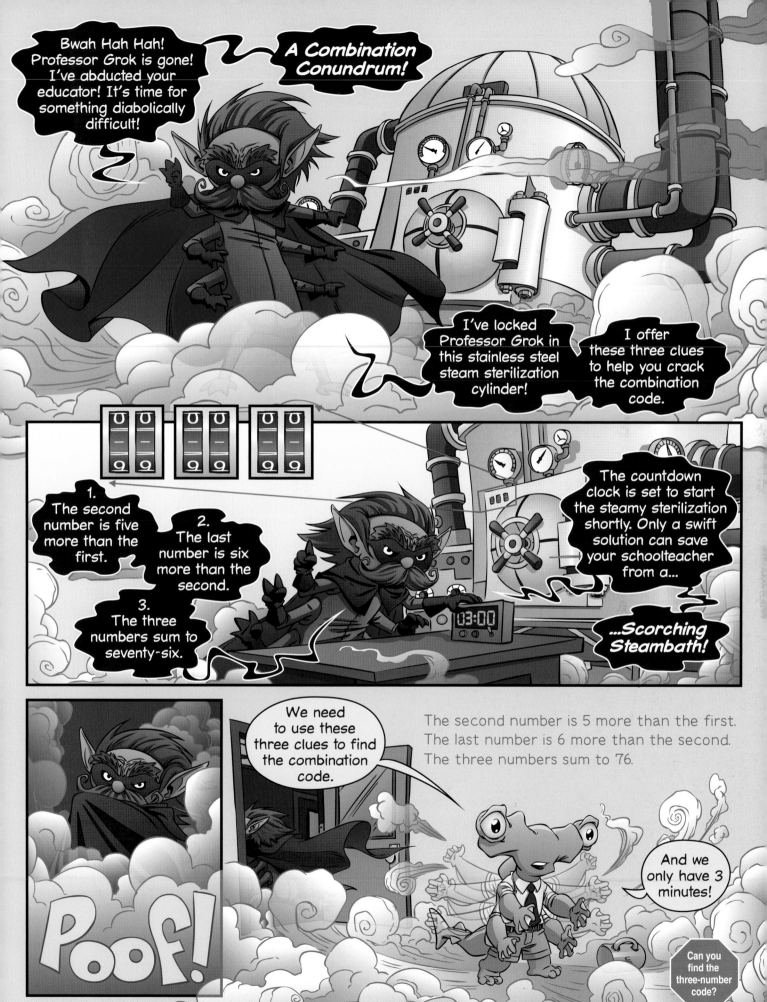

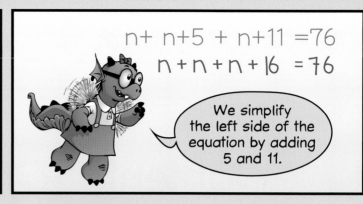

Practice: Pages 22-34

Contents: Chapter 8

See page 36 in the Practice book for a recommended reading/practice sequence for Chapter 8.

Chapter 8:
Division

45

I can separate the 36 stamps into piles of three, and see how many piles of stamps there are.

Let's see...

3 6 9 12 15 18 21 24 27 30 33 36 stamps.

That's 12 piles of 3!

12 monsters can share 36 stamps if each monster gets 3 stamps.

We can solve two types of problems with division!

What do you mean, Winnie?

We can use division to find the number of *objects* in each pile.

Or, we can find the number of *piles*.

51

MATH TEAM
Leftovers

Who wants *pizza?!*

How many slices do we get?

I brought two pizzas, and each pizza has eight slices.

That's 2×8=16 slices!

Perfect! There are four of us, so we can each have 16÷4=4 slices!

Let's eat!

Ahem.

There are *five* of us. You forgot about Fiona!

Oh, right.

We need to divide the 16 slices between the *five* of us.

16÷5 = ???

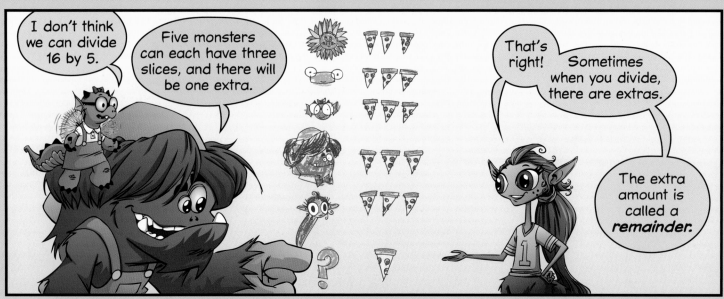

I don't think we can divide 16 by 5.

Five monsters can each have three slices, and there will be one extra.

That's right! Sometimes when you divide, there are extras.

The extra amount is called a **remainder**.

Division problems can be written like this:

$16 \div 5$

Sixteen is the number you are dividing. It is called the **dividend.**

Five is the number you are dividing by. It is called the **divisor.**

$16 \div 5$

We can write the same division problem like this:

$5 \overline{)16}$

It means the same thing as 16÷5, but we usually think of it as "How many times does five *go into* sixteen?"

WHEN WE ASK HOW MANY TIMES FIVE "GOES INTO" SIXTEEN, WE ARE ASKING HOW MANY FIVES CAN BE ADDED WITHOUT GOING OVER SIXTEEN.

Five goes into sixteen three times.

Three is called the *quotient*.

3
5)16

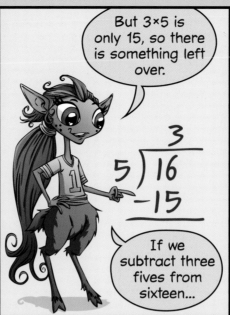

But 3×5 is only 15, so there is something left over.

3
5)16
-15

If we subtract three fives from sixteen...

...there is one extra.

3
5)16
-15
1

THIS PROCESS IS CALLED *LONG DIVISION*.

When we divide 16 by 5, we get a *quotient* of 3 and a *remainder* of 1.

When we use long division, we count how many times we can subtract the *divisor* from the *dividend*...

...and keep track of the extras.

Try it!

If 30 cookies are divided equally among 7 monsters, how many extra cookies will there be?

Solve it!

We need to divide 30 by 7.

7)30

Since 7×4=28, seven goes into 30 *four* times.

4
7)30

55

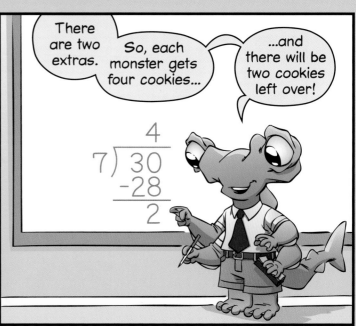

$$7 \times 4 = 28$$

$$28 + 2 = 30$$

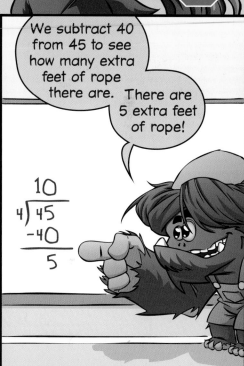

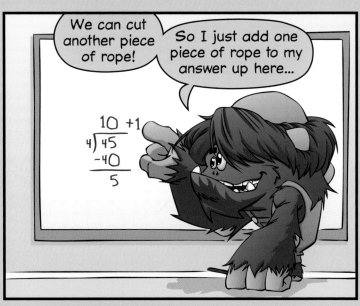

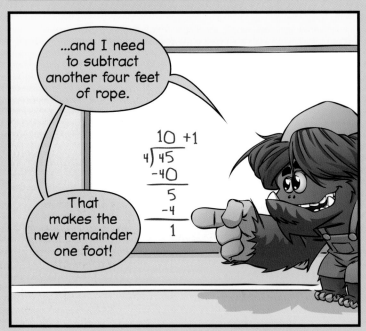

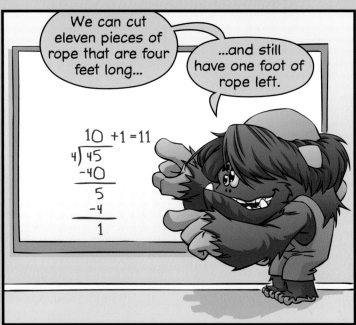

58

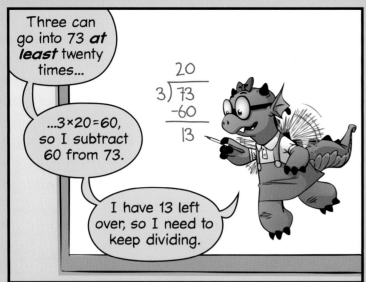

Three can go into 73 **at least** twenty times...

...3×20=60, so I subtract 60 from 73.

I have 13 left over, so I need to keep dividing.

$$
\begin{array}{r}
20 \\
3\overline{)73} \\
-60 \\
\hline
13
\end{array}
$$

Three goes into 13 four times, so I add four to the quotient.

$$
\begin{array}{r}
20 \;+4 \\
3\overline{)73} \\
-60 \\
\hline
13
\end{array}
$$

And I need to subtract four more threes, which is 12.

$$
\begin{array}{r}
20 \;+4 \\
3\overline{)73} \\
-60 \\
\hline
13 \\
-12
\end{array}
$$

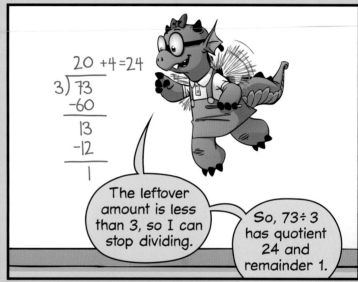

$$
\begin{array}{r}
20 \;+4 =24 \\
3\overline{)73} \\
-60 \\
\hline
13 \\
-12 \\
\hline
1
\end{array}
$$

The leftover amount is less than 3, so I can stop dividing.

So, 73÷3 has quotient 24 and remainder 1.

Speaking of leftovers...

...what happened to the extra slice of pizza?

Look what I found!

Free pizza!

$89 \div 7$ means the same thing as $7\overline{)89}$

dividend   divisor   divisor   dividend

To divide 89 by 7 using long division:

$7\overline{)89}$ First, guess how many times 7 can go into 89.
                 If you guess too high, start over.
                 $7 \times 10 = 70$, so 7 goes into 89 at least 10 times.

$\begin{array}{r} 10 \\ 7\overline{)89} \\ -70 \\ \hline 19 \end{array}$ ← The 10 goes here. This is where we keep
                 track of how many 7's we've subtracted.
                 ← Subtract ten 7's ($10 \times 7 = 70$) from 89.
                 This leaves 19.
                 Since 19 is bigger than 7, we can subtract
                 more 7's.

$\begin{array}{r} 10+2 \\ 7\overline{)89} \\ -70 \\ \hline 19 \\ -14 \\ \hline 5 \end{array}$ ← 7 goes into 19 two times,
                 so we add two up here.

                 ← We subtract $2 \times 7 = 14$ to get 5.
                 Since 5 is less than 7, we can't
                 subtract any more 7's.

$\begin{array}{r} 10+2=\boxed{12} \\ 7\overline{)89} \\ -70 \\ \hline 19 \\ -14 \\ \hline \boxed{5} \end{array}$ ← All together, we subtracted $10+2=12$ sevens.
                 The number of 7's we subtracted is
                 called the quotient.

                 ← The leftover is called the remainder.
                 So, $89 \div 7$ has quotient 12 and remainder 5.

Check: $12 \times 7 + 5 = 84 + 5 = 89$ ✓

*ONE DOZEN MEANS 12. A BAKER'S DOZEN HAS ONE EXTRA (13).

There are five extras.

That's right!

How did you do that so fast?

Instead of adding 12+12+12+13 and dividing by 11, I just added 1+1+1+2!

?!?

I added up each monster's leftovers.

If Yerg, Drew, and Plunk each share their 12 donuts between 11 students, they will each have one extra.

And if Sally shares her 13 donuts, she will have two extra.

That's a total of 1+1+1+2=5 extra donuts!

Instead of adding all the donuts *then* finding the remainder...

...we can find the remainders and add them!

1

+1

+1

+2

= 5!

Very good! Sometimes it's faster that way!

Try finding the remainder when 9+9+11+12+12 is divided by 8.

FIND THE REMAINDER WHEN
9+9+11+12+12 IS DIVIDED BY 8.

Try it!

We can find the remainders first, then add them.

The remainder when 9 is divided by 8 is 1.

The remainder for 11 is 3.

And the remainder for 12 is 4.

Instead of adding 9+9+11+12+12, we can add 1+1+3+4+4.

The remainder is 13!

Wait. We can't have a remainder of 13 when we divide by 8.

The remainder has to be less than the divisor.

I know! What if we make the problem about donuts, like the last one?

HOw many extras are there

~~FIND THE REMAINDER~~ WHEN

9+9+11+12+12 ~~IS~~ DIVIDED BY 8.

dOnuts are   mOnsters

Now I can make a drawing!

I get it! We *can* add the remainders! But then we need to find the remainder of the remainders!

?!?

?!?

?!?

When we add the remainders, we get 13 extra donuts. But, there are 8 monsters.

We can give each monster one more donut!

Then there will only be 13−8= *5 left!*

Got it. We can take 8 of the extras and give one to each monster.

So instead of 13, the remainder is 5.

65

66

Practice: Pages 60-69

PRACTICE	Work with a partner to solve the problem below. Explain your work.

Team Name: ~~Grinnie~~
~~Power Princess and~~
~~the Purple Furball~~
~~team Mega-awesome~~
Unicorn Explosion

1.   What is the remainder when 13×24 is divided by 7?

step 1: make the problem about donuts.

How many extra donuts are there when
13 boxes of 24 donuts are shared by 7 monsters?

step 2: Divide the boxes between the monsters.
How many extra boxes are there?
Find the remainder of 13÷7
If each monster gets 1 box, there will be
13-7=⑥ extra boxes.

step 3: Divide the donuts.
How many extra donuts are in each extra box?
Find the remainder of 24÷7.
If each monster eats 3 donuts, that's 3×7=21 donuts.
So, there are 24-21=③ extra donuts in each extra box.

step 4: Figure how many extra donuts are in all the extra boxes.
Multiply the remainders.
6 extra boxes times 3 extra donuts in each extra box
= ⑱ extra donuts.

step 5: since 18 is bigger than 7, each monster can have more
donuts!   Find the remainder of the remainder.
Each monster can have 2 more donuts. 7×2=14
That leaves 18-14=④ extra donuts. So, (13×24)÷7 has remainder 4.

RECESS

Nim is an ancient game with many variations. In each variation, players take turns removing stones from one or more piles. The variations below, in which all of the stones begin in one pile, are sometimes called "subtraction games."

5|2: The game begins with 5 stones or other objects. Players take turns removing 1 or 2 stones. The player who picks up the last stone wins. The first player can always win if he or she plays correctly. Should the first player remove 1 or 2 stones to guarantee a win?

8|3: The game begins with 8 stones, and players take turns removing 1, 2, or 3 stones. The player who picks up the last stone wins. This time, the second player can always win. Can you find a strategy that will allow the second player to win every time?

21|3: The game begins with 21 stones, and players take turns removing 1, 2, or 3 stones. The player who picks up the last stone wins. Can you discover whether it is better to play first or second? What is the winning strategy?

In each of the numbered versions above, the first number gives you the number of stones to begin with. The second number gives you the maximum number of stones a player may remove each turn.
Try your own variations.

Find a partner and play!

Find more Nim games and winning strategies at BeastAcademy.com.

69

Contents: Chapter 9

See page 70 in the Practice book for a recommended reading/practice sequence for Chapter 9.

Chapter 9: Measurement

*THERE ARE TWO KINDS OF OUNCES. THE OUNCES ON THE PREVIOUS PAGE ARE USED TO MEASURE WEIGHT. THE *FLUID OUNCES* ON THIS PAGE ARE FOR MEASURING VOLUME (HOW MUCH SPACE SOMETHING TAKES UP).

Customary Units   Lizzie

Unit (abbreviation)   Conversion

Weight
ounce (oz)
pound (lb) | 1 lb = 16 oz
ton | 1 ton = 2,000 lb

Length
inch (in)
foot (ft) | 1 ft = 12 in | 1 inch
yard (yd) | 1 yd = 3 ft
mile (mi) | 1 mi = 5,280 ft

Volume
fluid ounce (fl oz)
cup (c) | 1 c = 8 fl oz
pint (pt) | 1 pt = 2 c
quart (qt) | 1 qt = 2 pt
gallon (gal) | 1 gal = 4 qt

Time
second (sec)
minute (min) | 1 min = 60 sec
hour (hr) | 1 hr = 60 min
day | 1 day = 24 hr
week | 1 week = 7 days
month | 1 month has 28-31 days
decade | 1 decade = 10 years
century | 1 century = 100 years
millennium | 1 millennium = 1,000 years

The long hand on a clock moves this far every minute.

The short hand on a clock moves this far every hour.

Temperature
degree Fahrenheit (°F)
    Water freezes: 32 °F
    Water boils: 212 °F

84

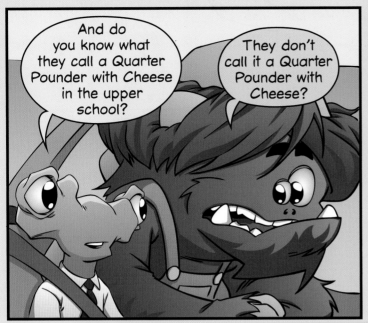

THE METRIC SYSTEM INCLUDES UNITS LIKE GRAMS, LITERS, AND METERS. IT IS THE STANDARD SYSTEM OF MEASUREMENT IN MOST OF THE WORLD, AND IS ALSO CALLED THE "INTERNATIONAL SYSTEM."

Before today's math meet, we are going to learn a whole new system of measurement!

Units are *so* annoying!

Why are there *twelve* inches in a foot, but only *three* feet in a yard?!

And *5,280* feet in a mile?! Why couldn't they just make a mile *5,000 feet?*

You kids are going to love the metric system...

...especially you, Alex.

In the metric system, length can be measured in centimeters, meters, and kilometers.

There are 100 centimeters in a meter...

...and 1,000 meters in a kilometer.

100 and 1,000...

...that's *awesome!*

THIS GRAY BOX IS ONE CENTIMETER TALL. ONE INCH IS A LITTLE MORE THAN TWO AND A HALF CENTIMETERS. ONE METER IS EQUAL TO 100 CENTIMETERS, WHICH IS A LITTLE MORE THAN 39 INCHES.

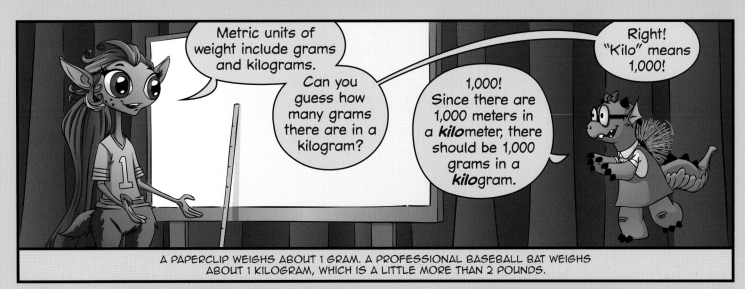

A PAPERCLIP WEIGHS ABOUT 1 GRAM. A PROFESSIONAL BASEBALL BAT WEIGHS ABOUT 1 KILOGRAM, WHICH IS A LITTLE MORE THAN 2 POUNDS.

FOR A LIST OF UNITS AND METRIC PREFIXES, SEE ALEX'S NOTES ON PAGE 100.

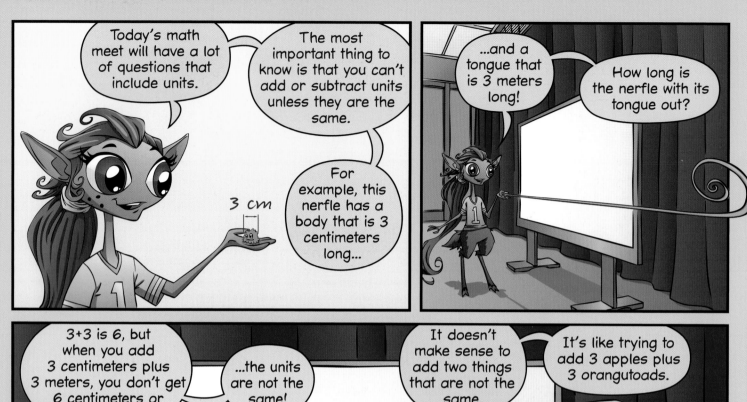

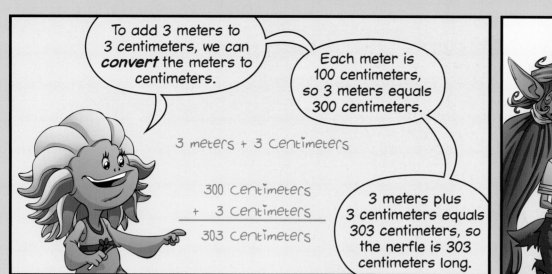

To add 3 meters to 3 centimeters, we can *convert* the meters to centimeters.

Each meter is 100 centimeters, so 3 meters equals 300 centimeters.

3 meters + 3 centimeters

$$\begin{array}{r} 300 \text{ centimeters} \\ + 3 \text{ centimeters} \\ \hline 303 \text{ centimeters} \end{array}$$

3 meters plus 3 centimeters equals 303 centimeters, so the nerfle is 303 centimeters long.

Great! How would you add 9 feet plus 2 yards?

What is 9 feet + 2 yards?

We can convert from yards to feet. Since one yard is three feet, 2 yards equals 2×3=6 feet.

1 yard = 3 feet

2 yards = 6 feet

9 feet + 2 yards
= 9 feet + 6 feet
= 15 feet

Then we can replace 2 yards with 6 feet and add. 9 feet plus 6 feet is 15 feet.

So 9 feet plus 2 yards is 15 feet.

Perfect.

And now...

It's starting, go out and take your spots!

...please welcome the Little Monsters of Beast Academy and their opponents... the Bots.

89

For today's math meet, we will ask six questions involving units. The first five are each worth one point, and the final question is worth two. The team with the most points wins the meet. Is everyone ready for the first question?

Question 1:
How many feet are there in 1 mile + 1 yard + 1 foot?

A mile is 5,280 feet, a yard is 3 feet, plus 1 foot is...

...5,280+3+1=

Ding!

5,284 feet!

Correct! The Little Monsters take the early lead, 1 to nothing.

Question 2:
It is now 9:50 a.m. What time will it be in 4 hours and 44 minutes?

We have to hurry, the bots have a clock!

We can add the hours first.

Try it!

In one hour, it will be 10:50 a.m.

In two hours, it will be 11:50 a.m.

In three hours, it will be 12:50 p.m.

And an hour after that, it will be 1:50 p.m.

We still have 44 minutes to add!

Ten minutes after 1:50, it will be 2:00 p.m.

That leaves just 44−10=34 minutes to add!

BZZZZZT!

2:34 p.m.

Correct! Bots tie the score: 1 to 1.

Question 3:
Sammy Snail slimes three meters in five minutes. How many centimeters can Sammy slime in six seconds?

First, we need to convert meters and minutes to centimeters and seconds.

Ding!

Do you know?

91

Question 5:
Plumber Pete cuts a 96-centimeter pipe into two pieces so that the long piece is 14 centimeters longer than the short piece. What is the length of the long piece of pipe?

Try it!

We need to find two numbers that add up to 96.

And one of the numbers has to be 14 more than the other.

We can use a variable!

Huh?

If we use p to represent the length of the short piece... ...we can use $p+14$ to represent the length of the long piece.

Because the long piece is 14 centimeters longer than the short piece!

P

P + 14

Right! And, if we put the two pieces together, we get a 96-centimeter pipe.

96

P   P + 14

Write an equation and solve for p.

94

$p + (p+14) = 96$

So, $p+(p+14)=96$

$p + p+14 = 96$

We don't need these parentheses.

$p + p+14 = 96$
$-14 \quad -14$

Now, we can subtract 14 from both sides of the equation.

$p + p+14 = 96$
$\underline{-14 \quad -14}$
$p + p \quad = 82$

If $p+p$ is 82, then p must be...

Ding!

41 centimeters!

I'm sorry, that answer is incorrect.

What was Grogg's mistake?

Grogg! The length of the **short** piece was p!

We needed to find the length of the **long** piece!

The **long** piece is 14 centimeters longer than the short piece...

...$p+14$!

BZNNT!

95

What be the best way to measure a roll of fabric to be divided among 9 pirates?

You could weigh it!

Weigh it?!

If the fabric weighs 18 pounds, and you want to give each pirate two pounds...

...how can you cut *fabric* into *two-pound pieces?!*

You should probably find the *length* of the fabric on the roll.

Aye, for a roll of fabric, we always find its length before dividin' the roll.

'Tis important to choose an appropriate measure.

For example, you don't measure apple cider by the foot, or by the pound.

Cider be measured by volume, usually in gallons.

And when ye be measurin' gold, weight be most important.

But items like rope 'n' fabric be measured by length.

102

103

106

We can be more accurate if we measure in ounces.

Right, because it's **close** to one pound...

...it might be a little more, or a little less.

Aye, 'tis more accurate to use ounces. There be 10 ounces of saffron in this jar.

YOU *COULD* MEASURE THE SAFFRON IN POUNDS, BUT YOU WOULD HAVE TO USE A FRACTION.
WE DISCUSS FRACTIONS IN BEAST ACADEMY 3D.

So, sometimes it's better to use a big unit.

If you ask my age, you probably want it in years, not minutes.

But small units can be more accurate.

If you want to know how long I can hold my breath, I should say "70 seconds," not "zero hours."

70 seconds! No one can hold their breath for 70 seconds.

I'll take that challenge.

Time us!

Practice: Pages 71-99

Want more Beast Academy?
Try Beast Academy Online!

Learn more at BeastAcademy.com